Just Because You Know It, Doesn't Make It Right

How to Paint a Prettier Picture for Your Life and Business

KATHRYN L. JACKSON

Manufactured in the United States of America.

Jackson, Kathryn
Just Because You know It, Doesn't Make It Right:
How to Paint a Prettier Picture of Your Life and Business
ISBN: 978-1-953586-07-0

Cover design by: Tyler Buse

Deja Hue Art
10505 S. Western Ave. Chicago, IL 60643

Visit our Website:
w w w . d e j a h u e a r t . c o m

CONTENTS

ACKNOWLEDGEMENT

First, I would like to thank my Lord and Savior Jesus Christ. I am forever grateful for the trials, as well as, the triumphs because the trials propelled me forward.

Thank you to my family who has pushed me when I needed it and humored me when my thoughts went way out of the box, but always there for support: Dexter & Mikela Jackson, Bryant & Keisha Thompson, Kevin & Natalie Murphy. My church family, Salem Baptist Church of Chicago. Special thanks to Eddie Davis and Devetta Smith for taking care of everything else, while I focused on the book and business.

I want to acknowledge my grandparents, who each sowed a special seed in me, to bring me to this point: Howard & Vera Melton, Bertram Holmes and Catherine Ferrell.

I want to take this opportunity to thank the people who have been supportive of me throughout this process and my life. I am so grateful for my editing team, who humbled me by not being afraid to tell me the truth. They are responsible for helping me put out a quality product: Eric & Sonya Bradley, Noelle Bradley, and Monique Dockery.

Last, but never least, I dedicate this book to my mother Jacqueline Johnson and my dad, Phillip Johnson. They not only gave me life but made sure that I was loved.

Thank You!

PREFACE

You know there is something more to life. There must be. So, you set out on a journey to find the exciting life you have always pictured. You visualized the life you wanted. You kept thinking positively. You followed all the success formulas from all the motivational speakers. After purchasing tons of books and watching hours of video, all you were left with was an average and ordinary existence and a library full of successful people living YOUR best life.

When you were born, there was so much hope for your future. Your parents believed that you were going to set the world on fire. Your family was so supportive. They told you, you could be anything you wanted to be.

As a child you start dreaming of what you want to be when you grow up. You wanted to be a movie star. You wanted to be an astronaut. You wanted to be president of the United States. As a child, you had big dreams of a big life. Now 20 years later, it's okay that you are not a movie star. You have your own YouTube channel. You no longer believe that you can be an astronaut, so you watch Star Wars movies on the weekend. You did not get to be president of the United States, but you are president of the local PTA. What happened to your dreams?

At what point did you decide to compromise? And how do you feel about the life that you are currently living? Does it line up with the picture that you had in your mind as a kid?

You went to school and got a "good job". You married your best friend and started a family. You went to church and you followed all the rules. Your picture-perfect life could not have been clearer. Now as you look in the mirror you find that the image in your mind does not line up with the reality that is your life.

Most girls picture their wedding day. You imagine meeting Prince Charming, who will love and cherish you and then together live happily ever after. You imagine a wedding day like in the movies. On this day, you get to be a real princess. You spent 15 or 20 years imagining the perfect day and dreaming of a perfect life with the man of your dreams.

When you meet someone and decide to get married, you spend at least a year planning the wedding day. It is at that point that some of the realities become more apparent. The picture on the canvas of your mind is vastly different than the realities before you. See in the fantasies as a child money was not an issue. In fact, money did not figure into the equation at all. You just imagined a fabulous wedding day. You never imagined that you would not be able to afford it.

Now the time has come, and you realize that weddings cost a lot of money. The designer dress you love is too expensive. You must trim the guest list, so that you can afford to pay for the reception. You must pay for wedding invitations, gifts for the bridal party, rehearsal dinner, the church, the tux, the flowers. You have so many expenses and none of them includes the cost of the honeymoon. The fabulous wedding day you envisioned, has you starting your new life in debt. That is not the picture you had in mind.

You work a job every day. Shouldn't you have enough money to pay for the things that you want? Not only are you employed but your espoused is also gainfully employed. So why do you have to compromise on the wedding day of your dreams? You have planned it for 15 years. Even before you knew who would be standing beside you. But now you are here, and you cannot afford it.

Unfortunately, this is only a glimpse into the reality that is now your life. See when you were a kid you dreamed of living in a huge house. You watched TV shows like the Brady Bunch, and you imagine that to be your family. The real problem is that you have done everything that you know how to do but everything you have done is not enough. You work hard every single day which is what you were taught. You went to school and you got a degree. You started at the bottom and worked your way to the top. As you look at the future of your current job, there is no apparent way for you to acquire wealth.

Jobs only pay you enough money to keep you coming back week after week. It is not designed for you to become wealthy. It really makes no sense that people keep following this same plan expecting a different result. They told you that if you go to school and get a job and work hard that you would have financial independence. Well you are 20 years into your career and that has yet to happen. Are you willing to give it another 20 years? Most people do. You go to work, day in day out believing that you are going to get ahead one day. Then at some point, without fanfare, you settle for mediocrity.

You no longer are trying to amass wealth and live an abundant life. You have now settled for getting to retirement. So that when you get to retirement you can take a percentage of what you used to make to continue living in the world where inflation is constant. Somehow you have been taught that that is the way to get through life. You still believe that one day you will get ahead and live a life of abundance. The interesting thing is that this fantasy has been peddled generation after generation after generation. It is like believing in Santa Claus. When you are young it is OK. You look forward to Christmas where you are going to get all the presents from this unknown guy who is just generous and giving out presents to kids all over the world. That is equivalent to what we are taught on how to get ahead in America through the system that is in place. Through education and through working a job. You never took the time to really examine the game plan that was given to you. See this game plan has been passed down from generation to generation and no one has questioned it.

Deep down in your soul you know that you should be doing better. You know that you can make an impact on the world. You know that your life should be greater. What you do not know is how to change it. Because no one has taught you how. See, you do what you do because of what you were taught even, if it no longer serves you.

The question is "Why do you do it?" One reason, you do not know any other way. Everyone in your circle lives life the same way, so there are no examples for you to follow on how to break the cycle.

I grew up in a poor neighborhood on the South side of Chicago. The thing is I did not realize that I was poor because everyone in my circle lived pretty much the same way. We did not own homes. We lived in apartment buildings. Our parents worked 9 to 5. We were what they call latchkey kids. We came home from school, entered our apartments with our keys, and we stayed there until our parents came home from work. We did not have a car. We used public transportation. We had food on our table every night and enough clothes for day to day living. We could not afford the most expensive clothes, but then no one in our circle had expensive clothes so we all fit in. My parents struggled financially, but they made sure that we always had what we needed.

It was not until I went away to college that I realized that I was poor. This was the first time that I was exposed to people of means outside of television. I had a group of friends who were African American like me, but they came from middle-class families. Some of them had cars on campus. Out of my group of friends, I was the only one in college and working a job. They all had bank accounts and no jobs, while I had a job and no bank account. It was then that I realized that there was a different way to live, other than what I had been exposed to.

So now here you are living a life based on what you were taught. Unfortunately, that life is a life of lack and limitations. As hard as you work, you should be able to enjoy the amenities of life. You should be able to travel the world. You should be able to purchase the house that you want to live in. You should be able to send your kids to the colleges that they want to attend. You should be able to live debt free.

As hard as you work you should be able to provide your daughter with the wedding of her dreams. You should be able to purchase a safe vehicle for your teenagers as they embark upon driving. You should be able to take vacations and build peak experiences with your family whenever you choose.

You should not have to sacrifice the amenities of everyday living so that you can send your kids to private school. The alternative is to send them to the neighborhood public school, which is grossly underperforming. So, you put your dreams on hold, as any good parent would, so that you can take care of your children's future. But all you can give them is the same plan that was given you. Go to school, get a degree, and get a good job. That is how you get to live the American dream.

The problem is the system is not set up for you to come out ahead. The system that has been ingrained in you is not meant for you to thrive. It is only meant for you to survive.

Perhaps you know someone like Ann? Ann has worked on her job for more than 10 years. She has a bachelor's degree and she is very well experienced. She is qualified for the supervisor position at your company, but every time the opportunity arises for her to potentially be promoted, her job looks externally for someone to fill the role. The third time that they brought someone in, Ann found out that her new supervisor was the cousin of the vice president of the company.

When Ann voiced her concerns about not getting the role again, management accused her of being "bitter". They said that she had a bad attitude and was not a team player. They even suggested that she speak with the company psychologist. Ann spoke with the psychologist and he gave her a battery of tests. The result of the tests stated that the skills Ann brought to the table were in line with that of various CEOs of Fortune 500 companies. Based on the company psychologist's evaluation, she was highly underutilized, undervalued, and underpaid. Now this happened to someone that I know, but I guarantee you there is some version of this story that you can relate to yourself or to someone you know.

See, Corporate America can only grow if it has a workforce. If they taught everyone how to run a business of their own, they would not have anybody to work the business. They put all these rules in place, and they campaign and cleverly proselytize them so that we share them generation after generation as if they are gospel.

The problem is Corporate America does not follow these rules. The rules that they give to you are not the same rules that they follow. They are using a different play book.

You think that you know the right way to get ahead, because that is what you were taught, and people will fight to be right. People you trusted (mother, father, or grandparents) told you that this was the way. Go to school, get a job, and work your way up the ladder. Moving forward in a different direction would mean going against the grain of everything that the people you love, and respect taught you. But look at their lives. How are they living? Are they financially free? Are they able to leave a legacy for their family? Are they captains of industry?

You begin to settle for good enough. You have a job making $50,000 a year or maybe you make 75,000 or even $100,000, but you live in a house that cost you 40% of your income; the tuition for your children is another 20% of your income; car note, vacations, and all the amenities that you have use up the rest. You basically live from check to check and one emergency could be catastrophic financially.

To the outside world it looks like you have it all going on. You have a decent house. You have a high-end automobile. You save up all year to take the family on a vacation. You hang out with your friends and you watch TV. You go to concerts, movies, and shopping on the weekend. By all accounts, life looks pretty good.

Unfortunately, at any given moment, the company can lay you off. The company could file bankruptcy or move their operations overseas. For any number of reasons, the company can let you go and there is nothing that you can do about it. When you work for someone else, you are at their mercy and you build a life based on their promises. However, they can change directions and cancel their agreements of employment with you at any time. What happens to you and your family then?

What happened to your dreams? What did you really want to be when you grew up? It is a question often asked to kids, but we should be asking it to adults as well. Are you happy being a mailman? Are you excited about being an accountant or project manager? Do you like commuting to work, day in and day out? Do you like punching a clock? Do you like having to get permission to go to lunch or punch out early for the day or to plan a vacation for your family?

People have come to accept this type of living as the norm, because it's the way everyone else lives. It's just like when I was a kid and was poor but didn't know it, because everyone around me was also poor. Just because you know it, doesn't make it right. The rules Corporate America has set are not in your best interest. They are not meant to help you grow; they are designed to keep you dependent.

There is an old saying, 'Those who can, do; those who can't, teach'. This is how the myth of getting ahead is perpetuated generation after generation. Because the people who teach typically do not have real world experience. They went from school to school, meaning they graduated from school and went back into the education system as a teacher. Now they are sharing information with students about how to get ahead in the world when they have never actually done it. They start planting the seed of education being the way out of poverty from grade school and they continue through college.

So, you take their advice since they should be experts in the field, but their expertise only comes from a book. The books that have been written for academia are written to keep you in a suppressed state. They are not teaching you how to build wealth. They are not teaching you to excel. The education that you receive only teaches you to follow in the footsteps of the average person. The average person lives a life of mediocrity and lack.

You have an economics professor, teaching economics because that is the only thing he knows how to do. He can teach you about finances and how the economy works, but he is never actually applying those principles to his life to create wealth. The national average wage of an economist is $116,020, according to the Bureau of Labor Statistics. The starting salary of an economics professor is between $51,070–$72,400 per year. While these are livable wages, they are hardly setting the world on fire. Since the economics professor has not demonstrated that he can create wealth in the real world, how is he qualified to teach you? An economics teacher who is living check to check does not make sense. But people rarely question these norms. If he is truly knowledgeable about the economics of this world, why in the world is he working for someone else?

Even though I had very well-paying jobs; working in Corporate America has always been frustrating. When I looked for ways to get ahead, it always came back to getting more education. You have run into the same thing as well. I know because I see more students in their 40s and 50s going back to school to get a degree. The advertisement in the world is "you are never too old to learn" and they value life learners. People continue to go back to school to get another degree to get ahead. It is almost comical that we continue to fall for this.

When I was particularly fed up in one situation, I thought it might be prudent for me to go back and get a master's degree. My son was eight years old and the only way I could see to move my career forward as a manager was to get a master's degree. That is basically because I had been passed over more than once. So, I enrolled back in school in my late 30s and I took one marketing class. One day I was working on a paper while my son was sitting on the couch watching television. He asked me if I wanted to play a game of Monopoly with him. All I really wanted to do was to sit back and watch TV quietly because I had had a long day. But, I had a paper due, so, I had to spend that time writing the paper. I had to reject my son's offer to play a game, and I could not watch TV in peace. It was at that moment that I asked myself, "What are you doing?" I did not want to be a student at age 38. It was unfair to my child to be caught up in school, when education, in this season, should be focused on him.

The instructor was a genuinely nice lady and tried to encourage me to continue in my educational pursuits by sharing her story. She was an executive working at McDonald's. She worked her way up through the ranks from a retail store to corporate headquarters. While climbing the ladder, she took classes a few at a time. It took her 10 years to complete both her undergrad and post-secondary degree. Now she works as an adjunct professor in addition to her role at McDonald's. Her point was that it doesn't matter how long it takes, the important thing is that you finish. What I saw was a person who racked up financial debt getting her degrees and then had to work two jobs to make ends meet.

Here is the conundrum, at age 40, 50, sometimes even 60, people are reentering college at various levels. Whether it is to obtain a bachelor's, master's, or doctorate, the question is "Why"? Why would you dedicate so much time out of your life, at an age when you should be enjoying life, to obtaining another degree? It's because there is something missing in your life. There is some financial goal, most likely, that you have not attained and when you ask around and do the research to see how you can get ahead, the answer always goes back to "get another degree". When you sign up for school to get the degree, you take out an enormous loan to pay for school. You now have another degree so you can qualify for a job making $10,000 a year more than what you were making. The problem is that now you owe $40,000 in student loans. Society highlights and celebrates the fact that you have another degree. The reality is that you have dug a bigger financial hole for yourself.

None of the people celebrating your accomplishment will help you to pay down the debt for your new degree.

The $10,000 that you got in your new promotion has now put you behind because you owe $40,000 that you may be paying the rest of your life. And for the record, student loans are never forgiven. The federal government will take repayment of student loans from your Social Security check if need be.

You know people who are highly educated, with all kinds of initials after their name. Yet they must get up and go to work every day just like you. They cannot afford to quit their jobs and they pray that the job does not quit them. That means they are not financially free. They are not going to work because they want to go to work, they are going to work because they must go to work.

These people followed the "Great American Blueprint". After graduation, they started working and went out and bought their first home. After all, we were taught that your home is an asset. However, their new asset is eating up a large portion of their new income and they are trying to figure out why they cannot save enough or get ahead financially.

It is because you followed what you were taught and did the only thing you knew. After all, it is what your parents and grandparents, teachers and clergy all told you was the way to success in life. But to be fair, they can only teach you what they know. Now you're frustrated. You do not like your job; you do not make enough to live the life you dreamt of and you do not see any way out.

You must get up early to get to work by a certain time if you want to keep your job. Your boss is an idiot but makes more money than you. Perhaps you own your own business. You left Corporate America to pursue your passion only to find that you spend more time doing financial statements, inventory and sales/marketing than working in your area of expertise.

You love the water and envision yourself traveling to all the beaches of the world. Unfortunately, you only get 2 weeks of vacation and one week must line up with the kid's spring break. You thought you would have a lot of money, but after the mortgage, utilities, tuition, and food bills, you find it's better to have a "staycation" for the second week. Your small business has turned into a self-employed job. You cannot take a vacation because if you are not there, your income comes to a screeching halt.

Since traveling and visiting the world's beaches has been put on hold for a while, taking a dip in the pool after a long workday is the next best thing. However, your pool belongs to the local health club and they are not inclined to wait for you to finish cooking, cleaning, and preparing for the next day. When the day is done you look forward to curling up to your significant other and releasing all the stresses of the day, only to be met with indifference and a bad attitude.

This is not the rosy picture you dreamt of as you were envisioning your life. You were promised a life of abundance, but it appears that is reserved for the "special people". Where is the magic pill? Why do some people get all the breaks? If following all the rules does not lead to a successful life, what does?

The missing link from all the motivational messages, manifestation mantras and meditation magic are plans for action. If you add action to any of these methods, you will start to see results.

If the picture in your mind does not line up with the reality of your situation, take a page from the artist's handbook and paint a prettier picture. When an artist decides to create a work of art, there is a process much like the process needed to create a happier and more productive business and life.

He starts with a blank canvas and a vision. The artist has a vision of what he wants the outcome to look like. He gathers all the supplies needed to create the picture: a pencil, eraser, brushes, paint, and water to clean the brushes. He draws an outline of the picture and decides on the colors. Once he starts creating the picture, he stops along the way and evaluates what he has done. If it all looks good, he continues down that path. If he has made a mistake in the outline, he erases it and starts again. If he made a mistake in the painting process, he rinses his brush and covers it once the original coat has dried. Once the foundation of the painting is complete, he adds in the small details to make it Pop! Then Voila! A masterpiece has been created and he celebrates by unveiling it to the world.

Creating a new picture for your life or business requires these same steps. You first need to envision the life that you want. Then assess the resources you have at your disposal, put together a plan to reach your goals and evaluate each step to make sure you are moving in the right direction. If you follow the plan and continue to adjust as needed, your life and business will start to look like what you imagined.

Everyone was put on this earth for a purpose. You are responsible for delivering on your dash. The dash is what they put on obituaries between your birthdate and your transition to the next life. God gave each of you a dash, with the expectation that you would live full out and accomplish your purpose. The question is, what are you going to do with it? The blueprint for each life is unique. You cannot deliver on your dash by following the blueprint that society drew for the masses.

Take your cue from the artist creating a masterpiece. A masterpiece is special because it is one of a kind. Artists understand that they view the world from a unique lens. The artist is the consummate entrepreneur. The Urban Dictionary defines an entrepreneur as someone who views the world differently. They have the audacity to drop their current job, relationships, and outdated family beliefs to pursue rich dreams. They want to impact their community and possibly the world. Entrepreneurs know the world is flawed and that their 9 to 5 is just not cutting it. They feel deeply that they were created for more. They want to live life on their own terms. They want to create choices for their family and enjoy the financial freedom.

Many of you feel the same way. Fear of being different or fear of failure or possibly fear of success has you suffering through a routine existence. You followed the plan that others created, and your life is vastly different than the way you imagined. You know deep inside that you were made for more. Now is the time to paint a prettier picture.

Once you make the decision to upgrade your life, the possibilities are endless. You will undoubtedly struggle to get it the way you want it, but you will be doing it on your own terms and with measured intention. It is a process. You must trust the process.

This book will show you the process for painting a prettier picture for your life and/or business. If you have a solid plan and you are willing to sacrifice, you can achieve much more than you already have. You can live a better life. You can have more money, more fun and feel better about yourself while doing it.

CHAPTER 1

Relax

"No pressure. Just relax and watch it happen."

—Bob Ross

Robert Norman Ross, affectionately known as Bob Ross was an American painter, art instructor and television host. He was the creator and host of *The Joy of Painting*, an instructional television program that aired from 1983 to 1994 on PBS in the United States and in Canada, Latin America and Europe. He is famous for his positive and uplifting quotes about art and life. Since we are going to follow the notes of an artist, what better role model than the original paint party coach, Bob Ross?

The first thing you need to do when drawing up new plans for your life or business is relax. The Urban Dictionary defines relaxation as, "The one thing in our lives that disappears sometime between middle school and freshman year that doesn't come back until we are old and wrinkly and have nothing to do but watch our grandchildren". You may find this difficult to do, especially when you have just come to the realization that your life is not the one you imagined, and changes need to be made.

When you were younger, you started with a blank canvas and you envisioned the man, woman, or partner that you would do life with forever. You knew the two of you would have a wonderful life and live happily ever after. You planned to have two awesome kids, lots of money, an amazing career, or your own business.

Here you are years later, and you and your life partner are divorced or maybe wishing you were. Your two little bundles of joy are the source of many sleepless nights. The house you imagined; you did not get it. All that money you thought you would have in the bank, a little short, aren't you? You are two years into owning your own business and have not made a dime. You did not pay yourself back a penny and you are deeply in debt because of it.

So, as you move toward creating a new picture, it is extremely easy to get stressed out. You do not want to make the same mistake twice or make even bigger ones. It is very natural to get scared and tense up because you are going to have to start doing things differently than you are used to; if you want a different result. When most people think about making changes, they get nervous, anxious, and so keyed up, that they physically and/or mentally close themselves off.

When artists begin creating a new work of art, their mind must be clear of clutter and focused on the task at hand. That is why art is such a relaxing outlet. It is impossible to worry about other things and create beauty at the same time. The human mind is enormously powerful, but it can only possess one thought at a time. You can switch between different kinds of thoughts very quickly but moving your ideas from your head to the canvas requires intentional focus. The byproduct is it takes your mind off your troubles.

Scott Barry Kaufman, a cognitive scientist and coauthor of *Wired to Create: Unraveling the Mysteries of the Creative Mind* did a study that "highlights the importance of relaxation for creative thinking". The research showed that 72% of people get their best ideas in the shower. "The relaxing, solitary, and non-judgmental shower environment may afford creative thinking by allowing the mind to wander freely and causing people to be more open to their inner stream of consciousness and daydreams."

You start by relaxing. Take a breath. Find a private space and carve out some quiet time and ask yourself "What do I really want"? When you get still and quiet, your inner spirit will speak to you. It will tell you things that are, things that have been and things that are to come.

While meditating in the summer of 2019, something in my spirit told me to buy a new couch. It was an extraordinarily strong urging to go out and purchase a couch that weekend.

My lifestyle was so busy at that time that I barely did anything at home and I certainly did not spend much time on my couch. Home was strictly for refueling and sleeping.

My couch had seen better days, but since it was not being used all that much, I really did not have a desire to spend money to replace it. It just was not a priority for me at the time. However, I decided to follow the voice inside of me, and I went out and I purchased a new couch.

I bought a sectional with reclining chairs, cup holders, charging ports and a chaise lounge. This is the kind of couch that I had wanted for many years, so I was happy with the purchase. However, I still did not understand the need to purchase it at that time.

Seven months later, the coronavirus pandemic set in. Not only was the State of Illinois required to shelter in place, but most of the nation as well. I found myself, spending hours upon hours on my couch broadcasting webinars, hosting virtual paint parties and Facebook Live content. I was able to do it in comfort and without being embarrassed about the furniture in my house.

Your inner spirit will guide you if you take time to sit still and listen. But you also must trust yourself and take action. Had I not acted in August of 2019; it would have been too late for me to purchase a sofa when the virus hit in March of 2020. With the onslaught of the COVID-19 virus, I was laid off from my consulting job and Deja Hue Art's brick and mortar business came to a screeching halt. I would have been stuck broadcasting from an uncomfortable couch that I would have been embarrassed for the world to see. When you get still and quiet, life is revealed to you.

We live in such a fast-paced world where things are changing moment by moment. Relaxation has become a lost art. Below are some suggestions for uninterrupted quiet time to listen to your inner self and rediscover who you were meant to be.

Ideas for Relaxation:

A Hot Shower	Stretching	Deep Breathing
Get a massage	Meditate/Pray	Do something Creative
Take a Walk	Play with a favorite pet	Read an uplifting book
Drink Herbal Tea	Listen to music	Write in a Journal

Schedule one or two days a week, to start, for relaxation. Write down those times here and then put them in your planner. Plan at least 15 minutes and write down the activity you will engage in to help you unwind. If you can plan a few minutes every day, even better. This is a necessary activity because if you do not plan for self-care, the busyness of life will set in and you will forget to relax.

Days of the Week

_____

Specific Time of Day

_____

Relaxing Activity

_____

Now that you are relaxed. Get a picture in your mind of the ideal perfect day in your life. Do not just casually think about it and then throw it away because at the moment it seems impossible.

What would that look like if everything that you can think of works in your favor?

First, think about where you would be. Are you on a beach lying in a lounge chair with your favorite drink in hand? Are you on a yacht on a beautiful sunny day? Are you in the mountains in a log cabin with a roaring fire, drinking hot chocolate? Are you in a villa looking out at the Indian Ocean? Or maybe in a desert oasis in Palm Springs. Could it be in the very home you live in with a few fabulous upgrades like an insane pool with waterfalls, a lazy river, and an outdoor kitchen? The vision is yours and yours alone. Just like no two artists can create the exact same picture, you are the only one who can imagine a perfect day for your life.

Take 15 minutes to write down what the ultimate perfect day looks like for you. Imagine that it is possible.

_____

_____

_____

_____

_____

_____

Then imagine you are celebrating a major milestone in your life. Think about the people you would most like to be there celebrating with you. Are your parents, siblings, and children there? How about your spouse and extended family? Of course, your friends and people who have supported you along the way. Maybe you would like to have people who doubted you as well? Think about people both past and present who would be so proud of you and you would be honored to share your victory with.

Take 10 minutes and write down all the people you want to celebrate with you.

_____	_____
_____	_____
_____	_____
_____	_____

When you get to that point in your life, imagine what your finances look like. Have you been able to pay off all your debt? Are you financially free? How much money have you saved? Are you still working a job or running a business day to day? Are you living off the dividends of your hard work and savvy investments?

How much money do you want to make and have in the bank to feel financially secure?

_____

_____

_____

_____

How do you look physically? Are you showing up as the best version of yourself? Are you eating healthy and exercising? Have you lost weight? Are you maintaining a healthy lifestyle? Since you are dreaming, are you eating all of your favorite foods and still able to maintain great health and a killer body? Is your hair exactly right and are you wearing clothes you never thought you could afford or fit? Why not? This is your dream.

Describe what the epitome of a healthy life looks like for you.

_____

_____

_____

_____

_____

What do your relationships with your parents, spouse and children look like? Do you have healthy relationships? Have you been able to talk to each other and heal old hurts? Do you look forward to spending quality time with family and friends? Are you able to put the love and relationship above any pettiness? Have you forgiven yourself for any wrongs you brought to the relationship? How well do you communicate with each other?

Describe the ideal relationship you want with those closest to you.

_____

_____

_____

_____

_____

_____

Imagine your dream home. What does it look like? Is it a huge mansion on sprawling acres of land with tennis courts, an indoor and outdoor pool and olive trees in the back? (Oh sorry, that's my dream house.) Does it have a swimming pool and spa? How many bedrooms and bathrooms are there? Do you want a game room or a movie theater? What are the amenities that would really make you happy? Do not limit yourself to what you think you can afford.

_____

_____

_____

_____

_____

_____

Get a picture in your mind of the car that you want to drive. What does it look like? What color is it? Is it a sports car or is it a coupe? Do you want a rare, exotic automobile or do you want an SUV in three or four different colors? Figure out what that looks like for you.

What is your dream car?

_____

_____

_____

What do you want to provide for your family? What gifts do you want to give your partner? What about your kids, what do you want for them? Are you wanting them to go to college? Do you want to set up a trust fund for your grandchildren? Do you want to buy them a house? Do you want to set them up in business?

How do you want to show up for your family?

_____

_____

_____

_____

_____

_____

Do you want your own business? If so, what does that business look like? What problem will you solve for people? Is it in the entertainment arena? Do you have an idea for a new way to do something people do every day? Do you have a special skill or talent that people would pay for? Do you have a hobby you want to pursue? It does not have to be unique; it just has to be uniquely you.

What is your gift to the world? It does not have to be monetary. (Ex: Your love is a gift that only you can give.)

_____

_____

_____

_____

_____

_____

How will you show up for your community? Think about the one problem in the world that bothers you the most. Do not worry if the answer is too big for you to solve alone. Just think about the impact on the community if that problem no longer existed. If there was a way for you to grow enough food so that no one would ever experience hunger?

If you could help educate people who show promise but cannot afford tuition. If you could wipe out homelessness and hopelessness. Maybe you cannot solve that problem for all the people in the world, but you might be able to make a world of difference for a few.

_____

_____

_____

_____

_____

_____

With a relaxed mind, think about every area of your life and what it would look like on the best day of your life. Really spend some time imagining what the ideal situation looks like for you, regardless of your current reality. Before an artist can fill up a blank canvas, he must first get a clear picture of what he wants to create. To turn your life or your business into a masterpiece, you have to first envision what that looks like to you.

Use the space below to capture any areas that may have been missed. Remember to dream in detail.

_____

_____

_____

_____

_____

_____

CHAPTER 2

Assess the Tools at Your Disposal

"All you need to paint is a few tools, a little instruction, and a vision in your mind."

—Bob Ross

What supplies does an artist need? What do they have to work with? An artist would need a blank canvas, paints, brushes, a cup of water, pencils, and erasers. It is important to notice that the artist only grabs the supplies necessary to paint a picture. Power tools are not needed to paint a picture, so it would be dumb for the artist to carry around a drill. A drill would destroy the very surface needed to create the masterpiece.

Some of you have drills in your life. Just like the artist, you need to do an assessment of the supplies and tools you have in your life and business. In your life you have good friends who are there for you, supplying you with good advice and encouragement. These are your Suppliers. Then you have those negative, "you can never do right" people there drilling a hole in every dream and good idea that you have. They pinpoint everything that could go wrong, wait on you to fail, and reinforce how stupid you were to ever think that you could.

Assess each person in your life and figure out which category they fit in. Make sure your inner circle consists of people who you trust and will support you through the ups and the downs. Those that are not for you, get rid of them right now. Dump them. They represent tools you do not need. An artist does not work with tools he does not need, and neither should you.

You do not have to confront the drills in your life and make an announcement that you are erasing them. Just get busy working on you and you will not have time to entertain the negative noise. Once you have reached the other side of that relationship, you may even wonder what the appeal was in the first place.

When I first opened the art studio, I had a person close to me constantly casting doubt on my ability to make it work. I considered this person a close friend and was incredibly surprised by their reaction. They kept saying that they hope that it lasts, because the paint and sip business is probably just a fad. They told me that it is best if you have a business that is essential, so that if the economy goes bad, you will still be able to survive. In reality, they did not support the business at all. Although they gave lip service support, they never even came by to see the studio.

I remember one Friday night this friend called me to ask how business was going, because they had just passed by the studio and saw that the lights were off. It seemed that they were not rooting for me at all. In fact, it really felt like they wanted me to fail. I assessed the situation and decided to move forward and create some distance between us. I never confronted the behavior. I just focused on growing the business and I stopped sharing information.

In year four, I was surprised that they reached out and asked me to host a party for their non-profit organization. After that, this person recommended me to some of their colleagues and I ended up getting quite a bit of business from them. We still maintain a connection, but the relationship has most definitely been put on a back burner in terms of importance. This person was a drill (tool) and I did not need anyone close to me drilling holes in my ideas and plans.

That is what artists do. When they are working on a piece, they are so involved in creating, they do not have time for anything else. All the negative energy from the world fades away in those moments. Their only thoughts are how they can beautify their canvas.

Suppliers (People that help)

_____

_____

_____

_____

_____

_____

Tools (People that drill a hole in your plans)

_____

_____

_____

_____

_____

What are some of the other supplies you have at your fingertips? You have the Internet that is full of good information, if you know where to look. You have coaches and mentors. There are great books out there. You can go to seminars and classes. It is amazing how many people have never read a book in the area that most interests them. You must take time to invest in your life and your business to make sure the picture you imagined is the one you end up with. Jim Rohn, Tony Robbins, and many other successful people often state that success leaves clues. Becoming an expert in the area you want to grow is what will put you ahead of the pack. If you want better relationships, more money, a successful career or healthier lifestyle, the way forward has already been laid out. It is up to you to spend time researching and developing yourself in that area.

Pick one area in your life that you want to improve. Find a book on the subject. Find a person leading the field in that area and research their life. Watch any videos that they have online and follow up on any books that they quote or people that they learn from. I know your life is busy and finding time to read might be a bit of a challenge. However, in this age of technology, you can order audio books and listen during commute times or before going to sleep at night. Start a new habit of reading something that will propel your life in the direction you want it to go, every day. If you are serious about painting a prettier picture for your life or business, you must become educated in your field.

Follow this outline to start the research and development process. Then do it again and again. Soon you will be the expert.

Book Title

_____

Industry Leader

_____

Books the Industry Leader Reads

_____

People the Industry Leader Follows

_____

Seminar or Workshop to Attend

_____

Notice the artists' supplies include an eraser. They need an eraser because everything they draw is not going to work the first time. Nothing works 100% of the time. When they make a mistake, they just erase it. They do not get upset about it. They do not cry about it. They do not blame somebody else and they do not spend a whole lot of time dwelling on the error. They simply erase it and move on.

You may have made mistakes in your relationship. Just because you got into an argument and you were petty or they were petty, you can go back and communicate your way through that. You can say. "I'm sorry. I take responsibility," and then go about fixing it. Erasers in life and business take a lot of different forms. An apology is a great eraser.

Communication can also be an eraser. For example, I was talking to a friend of mine over the phone one evening; and I was sharing with her that I had to purchase a computer because the one I was using was showing signs of slowing down. Now this was during the shelter in place pandemic era. Deja Hue Art studio was forced to move operations online. With the slowdown of the business, my friend blessed me with some money to help me keep things afloat. During this time, it was more important than ever that I be smart with money.

I bought a new computer because the one I was using was having some issues. It was imperative that I have a working computer to support the virtual paint parties. If the computer stopped working during a scheduled party, it would have been disastrous. So, I bit the bullet and I purchased a computer online.

Well when I told my friend I had to purchase a computer her response was, "Why?" I gave her all the explanations that I listed above, and her response was dead silence. I figured she did not quite get the urgency, so I went further into details, explaining my position. Still, nothing. I began to get a little upset at the fact that she was judging me. I was thinking, I did not ask her for any money, she voluntarily deposited it into my account. And just because she gave me money did not give her the right to judge me or make assumptions about my decision-making abilities.

I began to get very heated and felt the need to clarify things, so I called her name to change the direction of the conversation and get to the bottom of her disdain. After calling her name a couple of times, she groggily answered, and I suddenly realized she had fallen asleep and never heard any of my detailed explanations.

But what if we had not talked about it. I could have gotten off the phone quite upset mistakenly thinking that she was judging me. Now, that seems like a small thing and in the totality of the world, it is. However, that is an example of how miscommunications can start, and relationships of all sorts have ended for far less.

You too can erase the errors you have made in your life. If you are human, you have made mistakes. Rather than owning the issues, most people spend a lot of time crying about them or blaming somebody else. You whine about it and complain to your friends. You find a focus group that will circle up with you and all cry together about it. But the only thing that will make a difference is acknowledging the error and fixing it. Just like the artist, you get to use your erasers and start over.

If there are strained relationships in your personal or business life, make a note of those relationships here. List the issues you have. Decide whether they are important enough to have a conversation to clear the air or if you can choose to let go and move on. Then follow up accordingly.

CHAPTER 3

Draw an Outline

"Any way you want it to be, that's just right."

—Bob Ross

Another instrument at the artist's disposal is a pencil. The pencil is used to create an outline. Outlines are used to help organize the painting by creating shapes and patterns to follow. Have you created an outline for your life or your business? Most people have not. You know a business plan is an outline. A list of goals written down is an outline. Outlines are created by putting pencil to paper.

Sometimes when a novice comes into the sip and paint studio, they are so anxious to get going, they just start throwing paint on the canvas with no direction. They look at the scheduled painting and they are confident they can do it. Usually halfway through they look at their creations and realize they are off track.

If an artist just starts painting without an outline, a vision or a plan, the result would be a big mess. To be fair, every now and then, the mess can be saved and turned into a masterpiece, but the odds are not in their favor.

Many people fail in business and in life because they do not take the time to create an outline. They get excited about the vision and move forward without a plan because writing out the plan is time consuming, boring and slows down the momentum.

There is an old Latin expression, *Festina Lente*, which means "Hurry Slow". Working in an organized and methodical manner, is typically the most efficient way to accomplish a task. That is the "slow, fast" way. When you lay a foundation and follow a process, it usually produces a better, more sustainable outcome.

When you skip crucial steps in the process, like sketching an outline or writing out a plan, you waste more time having to go back and correct mistakes. That is the "fast slow" way.

One of the artists that I mentored had an opportunity to display her works in a local café. After spending time with the owner and watching the operations, she knew that the owner was in over her head and asked me if I could help her. The artist arranged a meeting for the two of us and after visiting the restaurant and talking with the owner, I understood the artist's concerns.

Like many new restaurant owners, she opened the café because she had a knack for cooking. Everyone in her family and all her friends praised her food and encouraged her to open her own restaurant. And so, she did.

She leased a space in an area where the community embraces small businesses. She remodeled the entire place impeccably. She purchased all the furniture and industrial equipment needed. She got all the licenses and permits. She purchased the food supplies, had a sign made and opened for business.

However, she did not have a business plan, nor had she really planned out the business strategy. She did not account for employees' salaries. She did not have job descriptions outlining their duties. She spent each week praying that she would make enough money for payroll. Because it was such an unstable situation, she had high turnover and often was the only one running the restaurant.

She spent day and night in the restaurant. She was the hostess and the waitress. She was the cashier and the prep cook. She was the server, the manager, human resources, and the janitorial staff. Her friends and family that encouraged her to open the business came by periodically to help, but most had their own jobs and families to care for. She could not afford to pay them a living wage, and they were not in a place financially to dedicate themselves to her venture full time. She was overwhelmed.

I offered to help her put a plan together and she was grateful. However, she had her mind set on the way she envisioned her café and was unwilling to adjust. She saw her business as an "International" food service and wanted to have options from various cultures. She had Mexican, Asian, Soul Food and American fare. She served breakfast, lunch, and dinner, along with a variety of desserts, six days a week.

She was so busy working the business, she could rarely find time to meet for an hour to discuss the plans. The couple of times we met, we discussed pairing down her menu, but she was hesitant to remove any items because she wanted to be prepared to meet all the requests of her customers.

I had suggested that perhaps she only open for lunch and dinner to meet customer needs during the busiest times of the day. This would give her time to prep for the next shift and work on business operations. However, she was concerned that there might be one or two customers that she would miss, and she could not afford to miss any business. Many of the customers that came by wanting to support the business, soon stopped coming because the service was just too slow.

She was unwilling to pare down her menu or modify her hours or restructure her strategy of being everything to everybody. She was too busy to work on her financials, so she really had no idea if she was making a profit or not. In the end, she was so committed to the vision she had of her restaurant, there was no way to help her. She was unwilling to create an outline. She just wanted to keep the restaurant open and move forward, hoping things would get better.

It was an impossible situation to manage. She held on as long as she could. One day, she reached a breaking point, and everything came crashing down. Her waitresses quit because she had them working 2-3 additional jobs and was sometimes late with payroll. The lunch crowd all but went away, because she could not service them in a timely manner. She did not have enough money to order the food that she needed to prepare for the week. Not only were her business finances in a shamble, but her personal finances had suffered as well.

This is an example of someone who had a vision and a skill, but she did not have a plan. Ending in bankruptcy, was not the picture she had painted for her business, but she started painting without an outline.

That is what has happened to most people in life. They start out with ideas and visions of what they want the canvas of their life to look like, but do not take the time to create an outline. They just dive right into the paint, without even taking stock of what color to use.

They want a picture that is mostly blue, yet they grabbed the red paint and kept going and going and now they do not understand why their life does not look the way they imagined. It is because they grab the wrong paint. They started creating the picture with no guidelines to follow. There was no structure. There was no outline.

Now there was another young lady who also wanted to start a restaurant as well. She went through a business incubator program and

I served as her mentor. She specialized in plant-based food. She was just getting started, did not have a lot of capital, did not have any experience managing a restaurant. She agreed to get proof of concept before investing in a restaurant. She tested her product by serving as a personal chef.

Her mission was to help people transition to a healthier diet plan by creating tasty plant-based alternatives. She would go to her client's homes and prepare a weeks' worth of meals and package it so they could just heat it and eat it.

Her clientele grew through referrals and she soon expanded to a catering service model. With a solid list of clients, she rented a commercial kitchen space where she could prepare meals in bulk and then deliver them to her clients on a weekly basis. She also began to cater parties and holiday events for a health conscience clientele.

When the pandemic of 2020 hit, and everyone was sheltered in place. This young lady was still able to continue her business because of the model she had created. She operated a pickup and delivery service for an essential product. Her clientele grew as a byproduct of the shelter in place order. More health conscious, busy executives were working from home. Suddenly, they were working full time jobs and working as full-time teachers for their kids as well. Having their meals prepared and delivered served as a lifeline and her business became even more essential.

In this tale of two restaurants, both were great cooks and had a vision of opening a restaurant. One implored the fast, slow route, by jumping in without a plan. Ultimately, she will have to start again if she is so inclined. It is possible that she can still have her dream, but now she will have to start over from scratch. The second chef is running a thriving business with minimal overhead and a steady clientele. She ultimately wants to open a café for plant-based eating. The plan is to let the business dictate the growth. When she opens, she will already have proof of concept, a following and experience servicing customers.

When the idea of opening a paint and sip first came to me, I did not think about creating a formal business plan. In fact, I was blissfully ignorant about it. I did however put together a plan to start Deja Hue Art. I did a lot of informal research. I went to several established studios, both franchises and independent operators and I took notes on how they ran the business. I made a list of all the supplies used and I paid attention to the differences in each studio. I noted what was a must have and what impressed me about how they did business.

Without knowing the terminology or having the academic knowledge, I was doing an informal SWOT Analysis of my soon to be competitors. A SWOT analysis helps you understand internal and external factors that can make or break your success toward your marketing goals. SWOT is an acronym for Strength, Weakness, Opportunities and Threats and it is a critical part of a business and marketing plan.

Below is the simple common-sense plan that I used to get started and you can use this as a basic guide for an idea you may want to turn into a business.

I. What is your product or service?

_____

_____

_____

II. Who is your Ideal Customer?

_____

_____

_____

_____

_____

III. Why do you believe this idea will work?

_____

_____

_____

_____

_____

IV. List all the materials needed and research the cost of each to start your business. (equipment, office supplies, etc.)

_____

_____

_____

_____

_____

V. Decide where you will do business and the cost to rent or buy, assuming it is not a home-based startup.

_____

_____

VI. Consider all the personnel you will need. Do you have the expertise to deliver on your product or service alone or will you need assistance? If you need assistance, how much will that cost?

_____

_____

_____

_____

VII. How much will you charge for your product or service? Do they line up with Industry standards?

_____

_____

_____

VIII. What sets you apart from everyone else? (Better service, more convenient, exclusivity)

_____

_____

_____

IX. How are you going to market your product or service?

_____

_____

_____

One week before Deja Hue Art had its grand opening, I thought it might be wise to take a business course. The traditional route would be to take the course first and then open the business, but I was thrust forward by enthusiasm. This was the epitome of throwing paint at the canvas with no structure.

In this program, the first crucial thing I learned was that I needed a marketing plan. Like most new business owners, I thought that "If we build it, they will come". Well that only works in the movies. You have got to understand who your ideal customer is, where they hang out and how they make decisions. New business owners don't know what they don't know, when it comes to marketing plans specifically and business plans in general.

Taking the business course proved to be the lifeline for Deja Hue's long-term success. The result of the course was a bonafide business plan, which I was able to use to get a loan. That loan allowed Deja Hue Art to go from a mobile operation to a brick and mortar studio. Had it not been for that course, Deja Hue would not have survived the first year of business.

If you are looking to solicit investors for your business, you will need a formal business plan. A business plan explains what your business does, your background, how you will operate and make a profit. It will also answer questions about why people should invest with you, how and when you will be able to pay them back. Below is an outline for a formal business plan. Business plans can vary depending on where you find them and the purpose. The business plan outline listed below contains the basics for any plan.

Basics of a Business Plan

- **Mission Statement**—An easy to remember statement illustrating a business' goals and purposes. The function is to guide you in making critical decisions that affect the direction of the company.
- **Business Concept**—Defines underlying goals (such as making a profit) and objectives. It should point out exactly what will be sold, to whom and why the business will hold a competitive edge.
- **Executive Summary**—Includes the major details of your report; It should grab the attention of the reader and let them know what you do and get them interested in reading the rest of your document.

- **Business Description**—This is an overview of the company. Includes:

  - Industry overview—provide information about current state and outlook of the industry
  - Opportunity—thorough description of the opportunity for your business in the marketplace; discuss what is currently missing and how your business will fill the gap
  - Mission Statement
  - Legal Structure
  - Business Location
  - Licenses/Permits/Registrations
  - Company Impact— describes the impact your company will have on your industry, customers, investors, and marketplace
  - Products/services
  - Distribution—describe manufacturing/distribution channels and support systems
  - Working Team—describe your staff and their qualifications and experience
  - Revenue—describe the funding needed to successfully start and expected repayment time frame. Includes loans, grants, donations expected ability to repay and sales projections

- **Financial Plan**—Determines whether the business idea is viable and a key component to attract investments in the idea. Includes:

  - Income Statement
  - Cash Flow Statement
  - Balance Sheet

- **Marketing Plan**—Everything you do to promote your business. Includes:

  - Market Research—summary of past, present and future changes in the market
  - Competitive Landscape—competition's strengths and weaknesses
  - Product Positioning—unique selling point, product features, consumer benefits
  - Target Market—demographics, psychographics, market size
  - Advertising Strategy—includes overview of media and timing and budget
  - Pricing—summarize pricing strategy and compare to similar products in the marketplace
  - Distribution—explain channels of distribution
  - Success Metrics—first 2–3 years' goals, requirements for success, measures of success/failure

Business plans are outlines that help entrepreneurs to see their way forward in business. Goals do the same for your life. Written goals can be considered an outline for your life. Just like the artist's outline, they keep you on task and moving forward. Written goals motivate your activity and create habits that will drive your performance.

Below are the results published by Damian Pros, June 30, 2015 in an online article, "*5 Reasons Why Writing Down Goals Increases the Odds of Achieving Them*".

Harvard's graduate students were asked if they have set clear, written goals for their futures, as well as if they have made specific plans to transform their fantasies into realities.

The result of the study was only 3 percent of the students had written goals and plans to accomplish them, 13 percent had goals in their minds but haven't written them anywhere and 84 percent had no goals at all.

Think for a moment which group you belong to.

After 10 years, the same group of students were interviewed again, and the conclusion of the study was totally astonishing.

The 13 percent of the class who had goals, but did not write them down, earned twice the amount of the 84 percent who had no goals.

The 3 percent who had written goals were earning, on average, 10 times as much as the other 97 percent of the class combined.

As you can see from the study, having goals, but not writing them down, takes you further than not having any goals at all. But having written goals puts you at the head of the class.

Additionally, goals help you to stay focused. When artists get lost in a painting, they refer to the outline to keep them on track. In life you are going to have obstacles that challenge you and get you off track. Having written down goals, can steer you back in the right direction. They help you when you are overwhelmed or feel stuck.

2020 was a year rifled with tragedies. First, there was the COVID-19 virus that spread worldwide. Hundreds of thousands of people died and millions were infected. George Floyd, an unarmed African American man was murdered by four policemen and it was captured on film. The world was outraged, and protests broke out nationwide. What started as peaceful protests, turned into rioting and looting. As a result, of these two tragedies, many people, including this author were overwhelmed with grief and loss.

For two full days I was unable to focus on my business. I was scheduled to launch a new workshop. The deadline for my book was due. The shelter in place was lifted in my state, so I needed to prepare the studio to reopen with new social distancing guidelines. My plate was full, but I was overwhelmed with sadness and disbelief of the crisis unfolding before my eyes. I was too traumatized to move. Nothing was getting accomplished.

I then did exactly what I have been sharing with you in this book. I spent some time in prayer. I got still and quiet for some time and listened to my inner spirit. My spirit reminded me that my strength was in planning. To move forward, I needed to outline a plan. Whenever you find yourself stuck, it's best to stick with what you know. What I know is how to put together a plan of action.

I implored a practice that I learned from a coach. I instituted my top 3 DIPs. DIP stands for Daily Intention Plan. I already had my long- and short-term goals in place. It was my daily actions that were in a state of paralysis. The thought of all the big goals in front of me and the current state of unrest, coupled with the constant changes in how we could do business, amidst these two major crises, overtook my mental ability to stay focused. By creating my top 3 DIPs each day, helped me to work my way out of the funk.

Each day I had an intention to accomplish three things. I recommend you add this formula to your daily action plans, and you will be amazed at how much you will accomplish and how good you will feel about yourself.

An example of my DIPs during this time:

1. **Find a way to help someone else.** When you help others, it takes your mind off your own problems. It reminds you that you are blessed and have contributions to make in the community and the world.

2. **Work on the biggest action that would directly increase revenue in my business.** If I were close to closing a deal, I would work on that first. If I needed to create kits and get them in the mail for an upcoming paint party, I focused on completing that. If nothing was on the books, I needed to make phone calls and send out emails promoting the next event. It was necessary that the business move forward even during a crisis.

3. **Close out 2–3 quick items of personal business, like pay a bill or order groceries.**

By accomplishing these 3 things each day, I was able to rest at night, knowing I was making progress. This helped me to center myself. I was accomplishing tasks step by step and removing the pressure of trying to get it all done at once. Art Williams, founder of A.L. Williams Insurance used to say, "All you can do, is all you can do. But all you can do is enough." After doing all I could do each day, I was able to rest easy at night.

I was uneasy about the state of the world, but not making progress in my business and personal life added even more stress. While I typically thrive in chaos, this period in history almost got the better of me. Because I had a plan, a plan is another form of an outline, I was able to refer to the plan to get my life and business back on track, just like the artist does. See, following the plan keeps you moving forward and making progress despite how you feel.

Not having your goals written down is equivalent to making a New Year's Resolution. New Year's resolutions are prime examples of what happens to goals that you keep in your head. Every year around December 31st, people resolve that they are going to lose weight, stop smoking and save more money. These are big sweeping goals that require a massive mindset shift. Most people believe that it takes 21 days to break an old habit or solidify a new one. However, studies show that on average it takes about 66 days. The average new year's resolution is typically broken within the first 13 days of the year.

Once you have your big goals set, write down your daily intentions and fill them with the most urgent activities each day. It's best if you do this every night before you go to bed. Planning for the next day helps you stay focused. This is especially helpful for entrepreneurs, because without a set schedule, it's amazingly easy to feel busy, but miss the critical tasks for the day.

Choose one of your visions from chapter one and list them below as a goal. If it is a big goal, break it down into bite size pieces and work on accomplishing it one step at a time.

Goal:

_____

Goal Completion Date:

_____

What is the Current State? (Be honest with yourself):

_____

_____

_____

_____

Action Steps Needed to make changes :

_____

_____

_____

_____

Available Resources:

_____

_____

_____

Possible Roadblocks:

_____

_____

_____

_____

Ways to Mitigate the Roadblocks:

_____

_____

_____

_____

Use this formula to write out your DIPs. It will change day to day. If you follow it, it will help you see immediate progress toward your goal. Following this formula will make you feel better about your life and business. As Tony Robbins always says, "Progress equals happiness".

1. How can I be of service today?

_____

_____

_____

2. What action can I take that will generate the most currency for me today?

_____

_____

_____

3. What urgent personal matters need my attention today?

_____

_____

_____

CHAPTER 4

Get Started

"Here's your bravery test!"

—Bob Ross

Once you get your outline drawn, the next step is the most important step. You must get started. It sounds simple, but this is where a lot of people get stuck.

For some people, getting started is the hardest part. You know what you want the picture to look like. You spend time dreaming about it and planning for it. You might have even written it down or put it on a vision board. But having a vision, assessing your resources, and getting the right supplies means nothing if you never get started.

Why do people hesitate to get started? There are some of you that suffer from "Analysis Paralysis". You have an analytical mind in which you look at all the possible outcomes of a situation. You are extremely intelligent. You weigh out the options of making a right turn, verses a left one. You look for every possible scenario and you weigh the pros and the cons. You see potential failure and success from all angles, and you have an innate need to make the right decision, based on the data.

Art Williams always says, "The problem with smart people is that they are so busy figuring things out, that they never actually get around to doing anything".

This is one of the main reasons that people stay in uncomfortable situations in their lives. They imagine the worst-case scenarios when they think of making a change. They decide that the devil they know is better than what might be. It is for this reason that countless people stay in a job that they hate. You hate getting up to go to work every day. You spend 50% of your day on Sunday, dreading Monday, because the hell you experience at work is coming.

I used to commute to work and consequently rode the train with the same group of ladies every week and the conversation was always the same. On Monday, they would console each other and say things like, "it's going to be alright; we're going to make it." Inevitably on Wednesday, someone would lighten everyone's spirit by reminding them that it was "Hump Day!" They would take solace in knowing there were only 2 more days they had to suffer through. And on Friday, everyone was smiling and laughing saying, "Thank God it's Friday!".

According to Forbes, Americans spend a third of their lives at work and 70% of the people are dissatisfied with their employment. So why do people continue to stay in a job they hate? Because you are doing what you have been taught. You were trained to get an education and then get a good job and you will live happily ever after. You now know from firsthand experience that is not true, but when you look at the alternatives, getting a better job or creating a business of your own, you decide a known hell is better than the unknown. You compare all the data. You know that there is a chance that where you go might be worse than where you are. It could also be better than where you are. You could be happier, have more money and more freedom. Rather than stepping out on faith you calculate the risk and decide to keep the status quo. You suffer from analysis paralysis and fear.

In life I have seen couples stay together because they believe that their current situation is the best that they could hope for. I know of a couple that lives together and have done so for years, even though the personal relationship is over. They sleep in separate bedrooms and they lead separate lives. However, when they go out in public, they hold hands and display affection. No one would ever guess that he has had numerous affairs, of which she is aware of and does not approve. She believes that good men are hard to find, so no use in trying. What she has with her husband is a stable home. He pays the bills, but she makes good money as well, so she is not beholden to him for financial survival. She has analyzed the possibilities and decided that leaving and seeking a better situation was just too risky. She was concerned that she may end up living alone or in a worse situation with a different man. When she looked at all the possible scenarios, she decided it was better to stay in a bad situation than take the risk of leaving in search of better. She clearly suffered from analysis paralysis coupled with low self-esteem and overshadowed by fear.

Fear is probably the biggest reason that some people never get started. Some people fear that they are going to mess up. They listen to their negative mental chatter. They do not want to make a mistake. As discussed earlier, in art and life, everything is workable. You will most likely make a mistake, but you can erase them. You can cover them. Or you can embrace them as part of the masterpiece.

One way to overcome the fear is to start speaking positive messages to tune out the negative ones. Faith comes by hearing. So, start listening to positive messages from external sources on a regular basis. Les Brown always says, "Anything worth doing is worth doing badly at first, until you learn to get better". Start speaking positivity into your own life. Life coaches often say you should talk to yourself like you would your best friend. If your best friend were afraid to do something, you would remind them how special they are and encourage them with kindness.

Speak positive words to yourself, out loud while looking in a mirror. It might seem silly at first, but the more you hear positive things about yourself, the more you begin to believe them. You cannot wait on the rest of the world to build you up. You must do it for yourself. Learn some of the self-development mantras like "Done is better than perfect" and "Good is good enough". Then move forward.

When I wanted to start my speaking career, my coach told me to start doing Facebook Live broadcasts. Two weeks had passed, and I had not moved forward with her advice. While on a group coaching call, she asked everyone how the Facebook Live presentations were going. Well, she knew that I was new to speaking and unlike many of my colleagues, I did not yet have many coaching clients. So, I very astutely reminded her that the reason I had not started doing Facebook Lives was because I did not have enough content.

Before I could finish my sentence, she gave me a "Bullshit Tech". She literally gave me the NBA Tech call, hand signals and all. She said, "Bullshit. You have more content than most people I know. You just want it to be perfect". As I sat with my mouth open in awe, she said, "do it ugly". Then she smiled at me, very sweetly and said "I'm so glad you are on this call. Now hang up and I want to see a Facebook Live from you this afternoon."

I was exhilarated at the fact that she thought I had content. I was in awe of the fact that she called me on my "Bullshit". I was terrified at the thought of doing a live broadcast. However, more than anything, I was determined not to let her down. So, I hung up the phone and I dug deep down in my lingerie drawer and found my big girl undies and did my first Facebook Live broadcast.

It was extremely ugly. I was clearly nervous. My voice was shaky, and I was a ball of nerves. Luckily, the only person that joined in was my good friend Patrice. I started with one of my most familiar stories and ended with some advice on moving forward even when you are scared. Patrice was incredibly supportive, and I called her afterwards to thank her. She let me know that what I said resonated with her. By the time the call ended, she had decided to move forward with a plan to reinvigorate her poetry writing skills and put them out into the world.

It was then that my confidence went up a notch or two. It was so gratifying to know that I had inspired someone. At that point I decided that if my voice inspires just one person, then developing my speaking platform was purposeful. So, I moved forward with Facebook live commentaries every weekday for 2 weeks straight. This led to *Coffee and Conversation with Me, Kathy Jackson* 3 days a week consistently and helped to build a large following. It would have never happened if I were not pushed to simply get started.

Some of you might be afraid that you are going to do well. The fear of success is a very real and common phobia. Some of you have experienced negative reactions from the people closest to you when you achieved a measure of success in the past. The trauma has left you scarred. When you achieved success, the people in your life who should have championed you, had their own issues and instead ridiculed you or somehow took the wind right out of your sails. Now you have a negatively charged emotional experience linked to achievement. So, all your life you have been choosing to stay under the radar and play small to help others feel more comfortable.

One of my favorite poems, *Our Deepest Fears*, by Marianne Williamson and made famous by Nelson Mandela, speaks directly to people who believe that playing small helps others feel good about themselves.

Our deepest fear is not that we are inadequate.
Our deepest fear is that we are powerful beyond measure.
It is our light, not our darkness
That most frightens us.

We ask ourselves
Who am I to be brilliant, gorgeous, talented, fabulous?
Actually, who are you not to be?
You are a child of God.

Your playing small
Does not serve the world.
There's nothing enlightened about shrinking
So that other people won't feel insecure around you.

We are all meant to shine,
As children do.
We were born to make manifest
The glory of God that is within us.

It's not just in some of us;
It's in everyone.

And as we let our own light shine,
We unconsciously give other people permission to do the same.

As we're liberated from our own fear,
Our presence automatically liberates others.

Perhaps you are afraid to do something well, because then there's pressure or perceived pressure of outdoing yourself the next go round. You are afraid the expectation that people will have of you, will be raised, because of what you have already accomplished. You are concerned you will not be able to sustain the success. Rather than setting an expectation that you believe you will not be able to duplicate or surpass, you choose not to get started at all.

When I started Deja Hue Art, I was not an artist. I figured I would just hire artists and let them lead the classes while I run the business. That worked well for a couple of years, until one day one of the artists did not show up. I had twenty-two women, drinking wine, and looking at me, ready to paint. I had left my phone at a party the night before and did not have a chance to retrieve it before this party started, so I could not call anyone for help. I became an artist in two hours. I had to draw upon my experience watching all the previous classes and a miracle from God to lead the class. One of my favorite scriptures says, "I can do all things through Christ who strengthens me." I have often said it, but that day, I lived it. I got my miracle, and everything turned out fine. The paintings were awesome, and the guest had a wonderful time.

After that experience, I realized that I needed to learn how to draw and paint so that I could lead classes if that ever happened again. So, I began to teach myself. I practiced tracing the pictures in my studio in my spare time and when I co-hosted parties with my artist, I practiced the drawings right along with the group. Soon, I was able to draw and paint every picture in my studio.

I could not draw or paint previously, because that was the story that I told myself. Once I got started, I learned that there was an artist in me all along. I started taking massive imperfect actions and eventually became amazingly comfortable leading classes.

The distance from a blank canvas to a masterpiece is consistent action. To create the picture that you want for your life and your business, starts with you taking imperfect, massive action. These actions are going to take you outside of your comfort zone. But what is the alternative? Do nothing and live with deep regrets?

When you decide to live a more productive and prosperous life, you are going to have to do some things differently. Stretch your comfort zone. The truth about comfort zones is that they are very pliable. They can enlarge to hold whatever you need them to hold. Have you ever heard of someone breaking their comfort zone? Have they ever been destroyed? No. You can only stretch them and when your comfort zones are stretched, you feel empowered and eventually at home in the new zone.

Think about a time when you were afraid to do something, but you did it anyway. Perhaps you were afraid the first time you scrambled eggs as a young person. You thought you might over cook it or under cook it or maybe set the whole house on fire. You worked past your fear and you got started. After you did it the first time, and nothing blew up, you were more comfortable doing it a second time and a third time. Each time you scrambled eggs they got better, and the process got easier. Suddenly, you were empowered not just to scramble eggs, now you are making omelets. Your comfort zone stretched once you acted.

When artists first start painting, they typically do not create masterpieces the first time out. They start with just painting one broad stroke.

Then they add another smaller stroke. The more strokes they paint the more they learn what each stroke does. They apply the techniques over and over and with each painting they get more confident. Then they get to a point that sitting at an easel and cranking out beautiful work of art is as natural as breathing.

Think about a time in your past when you had to learn something new. What were you feeling before getting started? Were you anxious, scared, excited? How did you feel once you conquered it? Take time and relive that experience in your mind. Write it out, so each time you get to a place in your life where you are afraid to get started, you can remember this event and remind yourself that you conquered that fear before.

_____

_____

_____

_____

_____

If you never get started. You will never know what could be. That is true in art, and in life. Maybe you wanted to write a book, but you never actually sit down and do it. You will live with a life full of regrets. You will never know how good it could have been. Not only would you suffer, but the world will suffer because the gifts that you have are not for you, they are for others. If you have a song or a poem inside of you and you do not sing it, the world suffers. If Marianne Williamson had not written that poem, Nelson Mandela would have never quoted it and millions of people, including this author, would not have been inspired.

If you do not climb Mount Everest, other people will not know that they can do it and the world suffers. Your gift is not for you it is for the masses. Perhaps the words in your book or song would have encouraged someone going through a similar ordeal. If you do not live your true purpose, people suffer.

Perhaps you have thought of an invention or came up with an improvement on an old one. If you have found a better, easier or a faster way to do something that people already do, put it out in the world. You need to move it forward, as soon as humanly possible. You don't want to take a pass and then a short time later see that someone else came up with the same idea, but they moved forward and now millions of people are grateful and as a result they have made millions of dollars.

Have you ever had a thought about how something could be improved, and then immediately talked yourself out of it because you did not know how to move it forward? Immediately, after coming up with the idea, you came up with all the reasons it would not work or that you were not equipped to pull it off? Most people have. If you do a certain task on a regular basis, a thought has probably crossed your mind as to how it can be done more efficiently or perhaps on a broader scale. These are the ideas that get you promoted on the job, help the community, and/or creates wealth for your family.

In the early 1980's, while standing on the bus stop heading to school, I came up with the idea of ride shares. Chicago winters can be very harsh. In zero degree weather your mind is forced to try to think of a better way forward. It was then that I thought how awesome it would be to have the then defunct Jitney Cab back in service.

In the 1950's, Jitney cabs rode up and down major thoroughfares carrying up to six passengers at a time for a fee. It was an unlicensed taxi business where citizens used their private cars for public transportation. They operated in high crime areas where the major cab companies refused to work. Immediately after having the thought of bringing back the Jitney Cab, my negative self-talk said "Nobody will get in a car with a stranger in today's day and age. And nobody would stop and pick up a stranger and give them a ride. It's just too dangerous". The idea was discarded as quickly as it came.

In 2009 Garrett Camp and Travis Kalanick founded Uber Cab Company, where people could hail a ride using their smartphones, from people driving their private cars. Today, the rideshare industry is worth billions of dollars. I missed out on revolutionizing the transportation industry because I did not believe in my idea. Talk about living with regrets.

Ideas and innovations come to you more often than you realize. You must be sensitive to your thoughts and be confident in your ability to move them forward. If you do not put them into the world, someone else will.

Think of some ways you can make life easier on your job, in your business or in your home. Maybe it is a new technique for exercising or a better way to potty train a toddler? Do not brush your ideas off. Explore the possibility of pushing them out into the world.

Opportunities are around you every day. You just need to train your brain to look for them. Start with these three questions.

1. What area in your life do you want to make easier (Cooking, exercising, smoother process at work, etc.)?
2. What about this process makes you angry? What is most irritating?
3. What invention or service could alleviate your pain?

List any ideas you have. Then list any potential obstacles. Then brainstorm ways to overcome those obstacles. The next step is the most important step. Getting started.

_____

_____

_____

_____

_____

_____

CHAPTER 5

Evaluation—Is your Picture turning out the way you had it in your Mind

"It's hard to see things when you are too close. Take a step back and look."
— Bob Ross

Now that the artists' picture is starting to take form, the artists will stop and evaluate their progress. This is where the artists concentrate most of their time. If they think that the picture is going well, then they continue down the path they are on. If they continue to successfully follow the outline and use the right colors, they will have a successful outcome. But if they feel like the picture is not going the way they envisioned it, this is the time to alter their course. Just like in life and business, you can always make changes. Everything is workable.

With paint, if you try to cover one color with another, while it is still wet, the colors will mix. To properly cover the old color, the artist must wait until the first coat is completely dry. This requires patience. Perhaps you wanted a blue background, but you used red paint. You can correct that, once the paint dries. If you try to cover it immediately and put blue paint over the red paint, it is going to mix and create purple. Sometimes the artist's mistake turns out to be the masterpiece and they decide to keep them.

In 1856, 18-year-old chemist William Perkin turned out to be quite the young prodigy, inventing synthetic dye and going on to help fight cancer. Only, dye was nowhere close to what he intended on making.

Perkin was working on creating an artificial version of the malaria drug quinine. Instead, his experiments produced a dark oily sludge. Not only did the sludge turn silk a striking shade of light purple, it didn't wash out and was more vibrant and brighter than the existing dyes on the market. Up to that point, dyes were made mostly of insects, mollusks, or plant material. As later chronicled in the book Mauve: How One Man Invented a Color That Changed the World, *by Simon Garfield, Perkin's invention of mauve coloring became the hit of the Paris and London fashion scenes; Queen Victoria even wore it to her daughter's wedding in 1858.*

Perkin's work with dyes inspired German bacteriologist Paul Ehrlich, who used the inventions to pioneer immunology and the first chemotherapy, eventually winning a Nobel Prize. BY TIM DONNELLY, INC.COM CONTRIBUTOR@TIMDONNELLY

Another accidental masterpiece is The Leaning Tower of Pisa in Italy. Because of a design flaw, the Leaning Tower of Pisa is one of Italy's most iconic landmarks. The foundation for the bell tower was laid down in the year 1173, but it took almost 200 years to complete because of the political climate. By the time the builders constructed the 3rd floor, the building started leaning. It was built on soft soil, so the foundation began to give way under the weight of the tower. For many years now, top engineers from all over the world have been contracted to figure out a way to stabilize the structure, while maintaining the lean which has made it a must see for tourists in Italy.

To make it more personal, perhaps your little bundles of joy were not at all planned. Let us not call them mistakes. They were unintentional little miracles. But now you cannot imagine life without them.

Have you ever gotten a haircut and it did not turn out like you imagined? But then, the unintended version complimented your face or style even better. In life and business, just like in art, the mistake can sometimes turn out to be the masterpiece.

However, if blue is truly what the artist wants, then he must let the paint dry before covering it. Once it dries, he can go over the red and the purple and get the painting back on the right track. It takes patience to create a new masterpiece, a new life, or a new business.

If you have taken the advice earlier in this book and envisioned a larger life for yourself and your family, you may be fired up and ready to make it happen. However, it is important to apply patience along with a strategic plan. Just like the artist must purposefully wait on the first coat to dry before covering up the mistake, you must do the same when charting a new course.

When I started Deja Hue Art, I was working fulltime as a Recruiting Consultant for a major commercial real estate firm. While I jumped into the art business with both feet, I still worked full time for the first three years I was in business. I worked on my corporate job full-time and I ran the business full-time. It was not until my consulting contract came to an end that I decided to put all my energy into growing my business. During those first three years, I was learning how to successfully manage a business, but needed the steady income from my job.

During that time, I was miserable on the job. Like many of you I wanted to quit every day. I worked from home 100% of the time and still did not want to go to work. This was pre-COVID-19; when most people still went into the office to work. You know it is time to leave when you work from home and still dread going to work. But it was important to be as strategic as possible because I was a single mom with a child preparing for college. I was concerned about how it would impact the original plan for my family.

It is not recommended that you read this book or attend a motivational seminar and go into work on Monday and resign from your job. Nor is it advisable to make a rash decision to blow up your current relationships because it is not perfect. When making life changing decisions, it is advisable to apply patience. You did not get to where you are in your career, business, or life overnight, neither should you make sweeping changes overnight. You can create a strategic plan immediately but take time to get clarity about the direction you want your life to take. Communicate with the people that will be impacted by the change so that they are not blindsided.

With your goal in mind, ask yourself how the changes will affect:

Your partner

_____

Your children

_____

Your finances

_____

Your time

_____

The evaluation phase is where true artists' grit show up. They may be tempted to throw in the towel when they review their work only to discover that they are not where they want to be. They evaluate what is needed to reach the desired outcome and clearly see the way forward is going to require a lot more work than they originally thought. It is easy to get discouraged and give up.

Lack of persistence is a major reason for failure in art, life, and business. Most people give up too soon. A breakthrough could be just around the corner. A true artist never judges their work during the evaluation phase. Giving up at this point would only ensure failure. Creating a masterpiece not only requires patience, but also determination.

I once worked with a young lady who wanted to start a shoe company. She was excited to start a company that focused on comfortable, but super stylish shoes for women. She joined a business incubator program and I was assigned to be her mentor. She had a great idea, but she had not done any of the leg work to start the business. I counseled her to do research on her competitors, but she was convinced there were none. Once she discovered that not only was there competition in that space, she learned how far away she was from creating the product and then getting the business up and running. She had a viable idea, but she lacked the discipline and determination to see it through. Rather than going through the process and building a good foundation for the business, she quit on herself and the business.

Far too many people give up on life and business in the evaluation stage. They realize that the dream requires hard work and dedication. You will have to stop and regroup and start again many times before you start seeing any fruit from your labor. You do not go from zero to greatness without paying dues. And you will never create a masterpiece if you quit.

The artist does not go from a blank canvas to a masterpiece with the snap of a finger. Society advertises that you can have it all and be an overnight success. Overnight success comes from working hard night over night, over night for many years.

You could argue that those amateur singers that win competitions like American Idol experience overnight success. However, if you research their backgrounds you will see the struggles they went through and the years of training and singing in talent shows and bar mitzvahs.

The 2020 American Idol winner was Samantha Diaz, better known as Just Sam. She was thrust into the spotlight because of her audition and subsequent performances, landing her the prestigious honor of becoming The American Idol. However, Just Sam practiced her craft in the streets of New York. She was an extremely popular subway singer. She spent her days going from train to train performing for whatever people were willing to donate. In 2018, there was a documentary on her life as a subway performer. She had been performing in the streets since she was in middle school.

Yes, she gained instant fame because of American Idol. However, she practiced her craft every day for years before her audition. Just Sam is the perfect example of how preparation meets opportunity and produces success. Once she exploded on the stage, it seemed like she was an overnight success. The truth is that she envisioned herself being on television singing and she took massive action and worked on her craft every day for many years.

Sometimes when the artist looks at the painting, they say Whoa! This is great! This is even better than I planned. Other times they may look at their painting and say Whoa! This needs a whole lot more time and attention to get it where it needs to be. Some will look at the picture and say Whoa, maybe a different picture would have been better. Maybe the picture you had in your mind was not the picture you really wanted.

Have you ever stopped and evaluated your life or business? Have you examined where you might have gotten off track? Perhaps you made a mistake in the outline? Maybe the measurements were off, or it was incomplete? Perhaps you grabbed the wrong color paint but continued with it hoping things would work out despite the error. Sometimes you can get so focused on the end results, that you do not monitor the steps in between. You want the promotion, or you want a relationship with that person, only to find you are not happy once you have achieved the goal. If you had stopped and did an evaluation along the way, you might have noticed the signs that you were not happy. You were just driven.

You thought you wanted to be a lawyer. You watched Perry Mason, Law and Order, The Practice and all your life you wanted to be a hot-shot lawyer like the ones on television. So, you go to law school and halfway through you find the research and reading anything but exciting. You look at job prospects only to find that Hot Shot Lawyer is not in the job description. You will spend your days reading torts and filing paperwork. It is not the picture you had imagined at all.

I say that jokingly, but a good friend of mine went to law school. After the first year, she was so bored with it she wanted to quit. However, she was the first person in her family to go to law school and everyone was so proud of her. She was so concerned about not letting them down, that she continued and received her law degree.   T h i s is a prime example of knowing that you grabbed the wrong color paint, but you kept going forward anyway.

Sometimes in business you act too quickly. Perhaps an employee did something you did not agree with and you decide to fire them. When the dust cleared you had a whole new set of problems. You now have a hole in the organization that you need to fill. While that employee may have made a mistake, perhaps it was more of a coachable moment than a last straw. You acted too quickly and now you must find and train someone from the ground up. A good rule of thumb is to manage your employees with the same mindset you use when training your children. When your children mess up, you do not get rid of them. You tell them to sit in their rooms for a little while until emotions calm down: theirs and yours. Then you go back and have a conversation with them. When you act too quickly, you usually end up with a bigger mess.

The evaluation phase is probably the longest part of creating the picture. You paint a little and then you stop and look at it. You evaluate your process and if needed, make changes. Sometimes you must wait on the paint to dry, before applying the change. You repeat this process several times along the way. You do not want to rush this phase or skip over it. In art and in life, it is amazing how many people go from start to finish without ever stopping to do an evaluation. They get to the end and then say, this is not what I wanted.

During the evaluation stage you must look at where you are and measure it against where you want to be. Make sure you are heading in the right direction before getting too far off course.

If you have been in business for 6 months and you have not made a dime, that is a clue that somethings wrong. Maybe your expenses are too high. Maybe you should be talking to more people. Maybe your messaging is off. Maybe your product or service is off. Perhaps you are going after the wrong market. You do not just go from start to failure. There are clues along the way. You do not go from start to success unless you make some mistakes along the way. You must ask yourself: What am I doing wrong? How can I correct it? What are the steps to correct it?

It is extremely easy to get stuck in the evaluation stage. If you are a perfectionist, the evaluation phase could stop you dead in your tracks. If you are a big picture person, you might skim through this phase and miss some important milestones.

It is at this stage that it might be necessary to get a coach. Someone on the outside that can encourage you and help you see things in a different way. Just like in sports, a coach for your life and business will help you perfect your delivery. Most successful people have coaches. Your knowledge skills and abilities have brought you to this phase in your life. At some point you will come to the end of your abilities and reach a plateau. Now you need to connect with someone who can usher you to the next level.

Michael Jordan is arguably the greatest basketball player in history. He played fifteen seasons in the NBA and won six championships and 5 MVP awards. Jordan started his career with the Chicago Bulls in 1984. Jordan gained a lot of fame and accolades for his athleticism. He even held the record of the most points ever scored in a play-off game. He scored 63 points against the Boston Celtics. However, it was not until Phil Jackson took over the helm as the head coach in 1989, that Michael Jordan and the Chicago Bulls started to have winning seasons and ultimately win 6 championships.

Many people debate whether the coach or the player is responsible for the win. It obviously takes both. However, Michael Jordan retired from basketball for the final time because the Bulls organization did not bring Phil Jackson back. Phil Jackson went on to later coach the Los Angeles Lakers and led them to 5 NBA championships.

As a person who never participated in organized sports, I was not aware of the need for coaches and as a result I stayed in the evaluation stage for quite a while. I tried several businesses before opening

Deja Hue Art. I owned a personalized children's book franchise, I sold waist cinchers and financial services and a myriad of other businesses, because I was never completely satisfied with Corporate America. Deep in my heart, I knew I was made for something bigger, so I kept trying new things. I implored the sink or swim method to my earlier ventures. I would jump in with both feet and figure out how to swim or eventually sink.

When I decided to open Deja Hue Art, it started with the Sink or Swim Methodology, but I evaluated all my other ventures and decided I really wanted this one to work. That is when I decided to join the business program. Having coaches advise and share their knowledge made all the difference. This time I started painting with the wrong color, just like before, but I let the paint dry and then covered it with the right color. It was the coaching that led me to making the right choices and resulting in a successful business venture.

CHAPTER 6

Make it POP

"You need the dark in order to show the light."

— Bob Ross

Once the artist has completed the major parts of the painting, he adds the POP! The pop is the little details that do not stand out at first glance, but they subtly draw your focus to various aspects of the masterpiece. You add these details after the foundation is laid to highlight certain areas of the painting. Adding the extras to make the painting pop, is the final step in creating a masterpiece.

When customers come into the studio for a party. They are excited to get started and inevitably someone wants to paint that one thing that stands out to them, first. Typically, what is most prominent, was painted on top of the foundation and then highlighted with a contrasting color. The contrasting color gives it the pop and adding the pop is the last step.

If you put the details in first, they get overshadowed, covered or they blend in and distort the colors. Instead of adding to the piece, the artist will spend more time trying to correct the errors. It is also very probable that they will get so caught up in the details, they never get around to completing the painting. "You need the dark in order to show the light."—Bob Ross

In life and in business, people sometimes want to start with the pop. Building a better life, a better business, a healthier lifestyle, or better relationship is a process. Following the process sets you up for success. Each step in the process is important, but it is just as important that you apply the steps at the appropriate time.

It is all too common for new entrepreneurs to spend all their resources on creating the perfect website. They do not believe they can start selling until they get the website right. The website is just the pop. Knowing that your product or service will sale, is far more critical to the sustainability of business.

Can you imagine spending thousands of dollars, creating a website, hiring a PR firm, and upgrading your social media pages, only to find out that you do not have a marketable product or service? That is painting the pop before the masterpiece. Unfortunately, this is an all too common approach among new and emerging business owners.

Putting the Pop before the foundation is typical for business owners who move forward without a plan. The lady with the international café from chapter three is a prime example of painting the pop first. She put all her resources into the cafe décor. When it came time to pay her essential workers, she ran out of money. She had a beautiful restaurant with all the bells and whistles, but she ultimately went bankrupt because she could not afford to pay her staff.

Some people treat their relationships the same way. They have a picture of how they want it to be and they want to get straight to the Pop without laying a foundation. It takes years of planning, evaluating, and covering with more paint before you get to the Pop in a marriage. If the relationship is worth it, you will do the necessary work to get to the Pop.

The Pop is after 37 years you find yourself quarantined together in a pandemic, and you would rather be with them than anyone else in the world. That does not happen in year one of a marriage. In the beginning you are bringing two independent lives under one roof. As much as you have learned about each other during the dating phase of the relationship, living together takes it to a much deeper level.

My son and his girlfriend decided to move in together and I had some concerns. I grew up in the church and I am still regularly active. I was taught that people should marry and not "shack". My concern was purely based on my belief system. It had nothing to do with his girlfriend or their relationship. In fact, I was secretly hoping their relationship would grow and one day she would be my bonus daughter. I was just hoping they would marry first and then move in together.

They had dated for 5 years and had known each other since they were 8 years old. They spent the better part of their dating relationship in 2 different states, while they attended separate universities. Upon graduation, his girlfriend received a job offer in North Carolina. They decided that they no longer wanted the long-distance relationship. So, they both relocated to North Carolina upon graduation and started their careers and life there.

I voiced my concern to a close friend, and she had a different perspective. She and her husband have been happily married 33 years. She told me that she believes every couple should live together for at least a year before they marry. Most people focus on the wedding day and the honeymoon. They fail to plan for the marriage and a long life together. You really get to know a person when you live with them. She noted there is a difference in having a disagreement, with the ability to go home and cool off, verses having to lay down and wake up together. You need to know how you will show up for each other when tough times come. Weathering the storms together is what creates those loving bonds. Going through a ceremony is just the Pop.

Not only did she think living together before marriage was a good idea, she said it should be mandatory. That way you know what you are signing up for, before committing to it legally.

In her scenario, the idea of marriage is the Pop. The wedding planning, the rings and the honeymoon are Pops. Living together and learning to adjust, support and tolerate each other is the foundation. So perhaps, if people who are planning to marry, were required to live together first, they would be able to make an informed decision on how they want to spend the rest of their lives. In theory it would decrease the divorce rate and improve the commitment and longevity of marriage.

Without a strong foundation, all the pop you experienced, the exchanging of rings, the wedding, the honeymoon, they get overshadowed when the tough times come. But if there is a strong commitment, a solid foundation, you can ride the storms together and come out greater on the other side. That is the real Pop.

Too many people want the sparkle, the perfection, the bow on the package right at the start. You do not put the bow on the package until you wrap the package. You do not wrap the package until you have the package. Building the foundation, adding additional color and creatively correcting errors is how you create the package. Adding the contrast colors to highlight your hard work, that is putting on the bow. The bow makes the package sparkle. The pop makes the masterpiece complete.

CHAPTER 7

Celebrate

"There's nothing in the world that breeds success like success."
—Bob Ross

When the artist has completed his Masterpiece, he celebrates. He has a showing. He invites friends and family and sometimes the public to a viewing. He makes a big production. He caters and drinks champagne and has a dramatic unveiling. After all, what good is success if you cannot enjoy it.

When you accomplish your goals, you should celebrate. Failure to recognize milestones and celebrate them could have a negative effect on your life. You will feel like your life is only about work and it can cause you to burn out. You become a workaholic and miss out on what matters most in life. That is why people celebrate anniversaries and birthdays. It is a time to sit back and take stock of all your hard work and celebrate with the people you care about and that care about you.

Creating a masterpiece is great, but it is not the most important thing in life. At the end of life, when you have done all you can do, what really matters are the relationships you have built. Have you ever heard anyone on their deathbed giving out assignments to complete projects that they did not get a chance to finish? When people can intentionally say their final words, it typically focuses on family, friends, and love. Having rich relationships is really what makes up an abundant life.

In the Deja Hue Art Studio, they celebrate by bringing everyone together for a group picture. All the artists with their newly created masterpieces. They take all kinds of pictures and videos and they blast them all over social media. The best part about the celebration is watching the smiles on everyone's face. They are celebrating their accomplishments, but more importantly, they are doing so with people they care about.

Most of our customers are novices. They come into the studio skeptical of their ability to create the painting. They really do not expect to complete a picture that they can be proud of. They echo the same sentiments that I shared with the first artist that led me through a painting. I told him that if he could make me an artist, he was good. I told him that I could not even draw stick people.

I laugh every single time one of the Deja Hue customers says that to me. I hear it from someone in practically every class. I smile and tell them not to worry. I have superpowers. I have the power to bring out their inner third grade artist and then I make a showing of releasing my superpowers over each of them. When they get to the celebration phase and they are more than pleased with their work, I give them the "I told you I have Superpowers" reminder.

Completing the painting makes them feel good. Are they perfect copies of the original? Of course not. I often repeat to them what an art teacher once told me. "If you want an exact replica, take a photo". In art, just like in life and business, it is your uniqueness that makes the masterpiece special. Everyone brings their own strengths and experiences to the canvas and to life.

It is amazing how people spend their whole life trying to fit in, when everyone was made to be uniquely different. You are programmed from birth to copy behaviors and belief systems, so you can fit in.

HR professionals are tasked with recruiting talent for the organizations for which they work. Somewhere in the early 2000's someone came up with the bright idea of interviewing people for a "Culture Fit". Companies literally weeded out candidates that did not mirror the culture of their organization. This was considered a great thing, because the company had a set of values that they wanted all employees to line up with. The idea was that only hiring people that resembled the picture they had in their minds, should make the new hire transition seamless for all involved. After only a few years of having these policies in place, the public understood the expectations and learned to represent themselves accordingly, at least in the interview phase.

The fallacy with this Cultural Fit philosophy is that it created a "Stepford Wife" model of how corporate executives wanted people to behave and stifled individuality and creativity. In case you are not familiar, The Stepford Wives was a movie released in 1975. It was about a small suburb where the women happily go about their housework - cleaning, doing laundry, and cooking gourmet meals - to please their husbands. They never complained or debated or offered any resistance. Their sole goal was to please their husbands. The men were able to create this environment by replacing the real women with identical robots. In the movie, it did not go over well once exposed and Corporate America eventually learned the same lesson.

A very conservative manufacturing company had an opening for an IT Professional to train the staff on emerging technologies. In the interview a young lady was very poised and polished. She dressed professionally and she had great experience. She was extremely qualified for the job and she answered all the culture fit questions to the team's satisfaction. She was subsequently hired for the job.

After a few months, members of the executive team were required to take an advanced Microsoft Excel course to increase their skills and the young lady that they hired was the instructor. The first day of the course she wore sandals, and it was noted she had a tattoo on her ankles. Now this was in the early part of the turn of the century and tattoos were considered taboo in the corporate world. But it was a modest symbol and easily coverable, so not really a big deal. The next day when the executives returned to class, they noticed another tattoo on the back of her neck, when she had pulled her hair up into a ponytail. When she removed her jacket, because it was warm in the classroom, it revealed an intricate design on one of her shoulders. The class was a 5-day course and each day revealed more tattoos.

The members of the executive team began to recall her interview and concluded that this was a vastly different person than the one they initially met. She very cleverly tattooed her body in areas that could be covered when seeking employment.

Whereas tattoos are considered art and are very much a part of the larger culture now, back then it would have been a reason to deem her not a culture fit. Conventional thinking was that people with tattoos were a part of the seedy underworld culture and therefore, not a fit for Corporate America.

Had she not been astute enough to conceal her tattoos, they would not have hired her, and it would have been a terrible disservice to everyone. She was great at what she did. She took a technical subject matter and made it engaging for non-technical people.

In a video ad for a coaching program by Danielle Leslie, she introduces a new terminology. Leslie suggests that your unique experiences are a culture add, not a culture fit.

Just like an artist, what you bring to the canvas will be different for each person. In a paint and sip party, there is a display picture and a professional artist, leading the group step by step to show them how to recreate the painting. Although everyone hears the same instructions, each person will end up with a unique portrait. No two will be the same. But it is the differences that make the paintings a masterpiece. They are all one of a kind original, that can never be duplicated. It is the Unique Selling Point (USP) that only one person could have brought into the world. Differences should be celebrated.

It is the same in life and in business. If you recall from the Basics of a Business Plan outline listed previously, it asks for your USP. When pitching your business to potential investors, you must be prepared to share how your business will stand out among your competitors. They want to know why someone would pass by similar organizations and do business with you. When you are in business, you must find a way to stand out in a crowded field.

It is the same in relationships. No one marries the person that reminds them of every other person they have dated. When choosing a life partner, you choose the person that is different from anyone else you ever met. They are special to you and they make you feel like no one else ever has. It is their uniqueness that is most attractive.

It is the individuality of a painting that makes it a masterpiece and that is what makes it valuable.

CHAPTER 8

Do it Again

"Anytime you learn, you gain."

—Bob Ross

In the end, artists do not always end up with the picture they had in their head. They may have veered off course. Or perhaps mid-way through, they changed their mind about how they wanted the picture to end up. They may have made a mistake with the colors and to course correct, changed the whole color scheme.

Art, like life and business is all about problem solving. Many of the customers that come through Deja Hue Art studio do not end up with the picture they imagined. However, they end up with the picture they are supposed to have. The one that represents who they are and how they show up in the world.

Some people excel at the outline phase. They draw a perfect sketch. The coordinates and the values of the line are exactly right. They are super excited, but when they start to add the paint, things do not go as planned. Others are challenged with the outline, but when they apply the paint, it all evens out.

Some people are good at one thing, while others excel in a different area. If you are a big picture person, a visionary, you might tend to overlook details. In life, just like in art, details connect all the dots and complete the picture. If you can identify with this trait, perhaps you should seek out vendors or contractors, to focus on the details. It would be beneficial for you to surround yourself with employees that excel in those areas. I once had a boss who told me, "If you have a chore that must be done and you really detest it, if you can afford it, pay someone else to do it". This is how partnerships are built, both personally and professionally.

As a busy mom and career professional, she struggled with keeping up with the laundry. She was a single mom with a demanding work schedule. Between commuting to work, chauffeuring her young son to his many activities cooking and helping with homework, laundry was always put on the back burner. She just could not find the time. She started dropping off her laundry in the morning before work and when she came back in the evening, the laundry was hung and neatly folded. All she had to do when she got home was put it away. It not only cleared her schedule a bit, it also cleared her head. While she was busy being a super mom, there was always a quiet gnawing in her mind, trying to figure when she could get to the laundry. Partnering with the laundry service, gave her peace of mind as well as clean clothes for the week.

What are some areas in your business or life where you fall short? Decide if it is an advantage for you to grow that skill or is it a task best left to professionals. List some areas in your relationship where you struggle. Decide if these are traits that you need to work on and improve or are these areas that your mate can complement you. Understanding your strengths and weaknesses, helps you to put a plan in place so that you can have a successful life and business.

Some of you still will not end up with the exact picture you envisioned. But be proud of the fact that you got it done. Be proud of the fact that you did not quit. You can always paint another picture. It does not mean that the first one was bad. It was just your first time. The same is true for your life. If your current reality does not look like the picture you planned, it's okay. You get to try it again.

Like Bob Ross says, *"Anytime you learn, you gain"*. Now you have some experience. Now you have some new knowledge. Now you live in a new comfort zone. Think about how differently parents raise a second or third child from the first. It is not a case of favoritism either way. After the first child, the parents have more hands-on experience. With the subsequent children they have a wealth of experience to draw from. In business you make a plethora of mistakes when you first start out. But the great thing is you get to erase them and start over as many times as you need to.

At any time, you can decide to change a miserable situation. The choice is yours. You can keep blaming your parents, the economy, the government or even the weather. It no longer matters how you got to where you are, what counts now are the actions you are willing to take. Your next decision is your most important decision.

The simple truth is, if you want to change your situation, all you need to do is decide. If you are broke, decide to make more money. If you are lonely, decide to meet new people. If you hate your job, decide to get another one or create your own. If your relationship is broken, decide to fix it or move on. Once you make the decision to change, change will come.

Deciding to do nothing is also a choice. It is a decision to stay in the status quo. The only reason anyone would choose to stay in a bad situation, is fear of a worse situation. When you decide to stay where you are, you are not avoiding pain, you have just decided to deal with it and hope it does not get worse. The thing is, your situation can and most likely will get worse, because you are letting someone else paint your picture. No one else can see your vision, nor can they design your future the way you want it.

Pretending that everything is simply fine, may have worked for you in the past, but if you have continued reading this far, it is primarily because you see something of yourself in this story. If this situation resonates with you on any level, the covers have already been pulled back and you cannot unlearn these truths.

I left a 20-year HR career and started Deja Hue Art, a paint and sip studio in Chicago. I had no artistic abilities whatsoever. I could not even draw stick people. All I had was an idea, a desire, and an open credit card. Deja Hue Art has successfully surpassed the 5-year threshold, where most new businesses typically fail. I have learned to draw, and paint and I teach others to do the same. Has it been easy? No, but it has been more than worth it.

The dash is short. Some people have longer dashes than others, but ultimately, you have a finite moment in time to impact the world. You have the tools you need to increase your world view and expand your comfort zone. Read more books, feed your soul with positivity, and surround yourself with quality people. Now that you have been enlightened, living an average and ordinary life is unacceptable. You were created to make an impact. By stepping out of the shadows and living a life of purpose, you will make more meaningful connections. You will become a person of influence. When you get to the other side of your dash, you will have made a difference.